GREAT ESCAPES

THE HOLOCAUST

Lila Perl

Website: www.marshallcavendish.us

This publication represents the opinions and views of the author based on Lila Perl's
knowledge and research. The information in this book serves as a general guide only. The author and
publisher have used their best efforts in preparing this book and disclaim liability rising directly and
indirectly from the use and application of this book.

Other Marshall Cavendish Offices:
Marshall Cavendish International (Asia) Private Limited, 1 New Industrial Road, Singapore 536196
• Marshall Cavendish International (Thailand) Co Ltd. 253 Asoke, 12th Flr, Sukhumvit 21 Road,
Klongtoey Nua, Wattana, Bangkok 10110, Thailand • Marshall Cavendish (Malaysia) Sdn Bhd,
Times Subang, Lot 46, Subang Hi-Tech Industrial Park, Batu Tiga, 40000 Shah Alam, Selangor Darul
Ehsan, Malaysia

Marshall Cavendish is a trademark of Times Publishing Limited

All websites were available and accurate when this book was sent to press.

Library of Congress Cataloging-in-Publication Data

Perl, Lila.
The Holocaust / Lila Perl.
p. cm. -- (Great escapes)
Summary: "Presents accounts of narrow escapes executed by oppressed
individuals and groups while illuminating social issues and the historical
background that led to the event known as the Holocaust"—Provided by
publisher.
Includes bibliographical references and index.
ISBN 978-1-60870-472-9 (print) — ISBN 978-1-60870-693-8 (ebook)
1. Holocaust, Jewish (1939-1945)—Juvenile literature. 2. Auschwitz
(Concentration camp)—Juvenile literature. 3. World War,
1939-1945—Concentration camps—Poland—Juvenile literature. 4.
Concentration camp inmates—Poland—Oswiecim—Juvenile literature. 5.
Concentration camp escapes—Poland—Oswiecim—Juvenile literature. 6. Vrba,
Rudolf—Juvenile literature. 7. Wetzler, Alfrid, 1918-1988—Juvenile
literature. I. Title. II. Series.

D804.34.P47 2012   940.53'18—dc22   2011001583

Senior Editor: Deborah Grahame-Smith
Publisher: Michelle Bisson
Art Director: Anahid Hamparian
Series Designer: Kay Petronio

Photo research by Linda Sykes

The photographs in this book are used by permission and through the courtesy of:
©Robert Harding Picture Library Ltd/Alamy: cover, 8, 20;©William Manning/Corbis: 1; ©EmmePi
Travel/Alamy: 4, 24; © Roger-Viollet/The Image Works: 7; ©Hyungwon Kang/ Reuters/Corbis:
11; The Image Works: 14; ©Frank Leonardt/epa/Corbis: 19; Yad Vashem/United States Holocaust
Memorial Museum: 22, 32, 34; JTB Photo Communications, Inc./Alamy: 25; ©akg-images/The
Image Works: 27; National Archives/United States Holocaust Memorial Museum: 30, 59; ©Interfoto/
Alamy: 35; ©Les Gibbon/Alamy: 40; Topham/The Image Works: 42, 64; Private Collection: 43; ©Ira
Nowinski/Corbis: 45; ©Stephen Lam/San Francisco Chronicle/ Corbis: 48; ©Reuters/Corbis: 52;
©Auschwitz Museum/AFP/Getty Images: 57.

Printed in Malaysia (T)
135642

CONTENTS

Watchtowers manned by armed guards surrounded Auschwitz, the Nazi concentration camp, where more than one million people died during World War II.

HIDING IN PLAIN SIGHT

Even in April, the weather in eastern Poland could be frosty. The date was April 10, 1944. The two young men had been crouching in their hideout for three days and nights. Shivering with fear as well as the cold, their bodies cramped and tense, they barely spoke to each other—and even then, never above a whisper.

Their hideout was dangerous because it could not be more obvious. It was a huge pile of notched wooden building planks. Inside the pile they had carved out a tiny space for themselves. But the pile was going to be dismantled any day now, and the planks would be used to build more long wooden barracks to hold new arrivals of concentration camp prisoners.

The men's hideout sat within the guarded gates of the notorious Nazi death camp known as Auschwitz. More than 1 million people—most of them Jews—would be murdered at Auschwitz by May 1945, when Adolf Hitler's Germany was defeated and the war in Europe ended. Auschwitz was only one of dozens of concentration and death camps in the Nazi network. Many prisoners died of starvation, disease, forced labor, beatings, hangings, and executions. But these deaths would not have been enough to fulfill the plans of Hitler and his generals: to exterminate all the Jews of Europe—and possibly elsewhere. In all, the Nazis would murder 6 million Jews and 5 million other civilians in what would come to be known as the Holocaust—a word derived from a Greek word meaning "wholly burnt" or "destroyed by fire."

Auschwitz's officers herded newly arrived prisoners— especially women, children, the elderly, and others not fit for work—into gas chambers, where victims were asphyxiated in a matter of minutes. Their bodies were then burned in ovens. Day and night, thick black smoke with a strangely sweet smell issued from the chimneys of the crematoria.

The two young men in the hideout had seen it all. Rudi, whose full name was Rudolf Vrba, was only nineteen, but he'd already been in the camp for nearly two years, since June 1942. Fred, Rudi's companion in the plan to escape, was twenty-five-year-old Alfred Wetzler, who had arrived at Auschwitz in April 1942. For Rudi and Fred, even if they managed to evade capture, escape did not simply mean personal freedom. After all they had experienced as prisoners of the Nazi regime, they had decided that it was their responsibility to tell the world about the killing machine at Auschwitz, as well as to warn the members of European Jewish councils of the danger that awaited their people.

Vrba and Wetzler were from Slovakia, the eastern part of Czechoslovakia, which Hitler declared an independent state under German protection in 1939. Ruled by a puppet dictator, Slovakia had become a miniature image of Nazi Germany, where Hitler came to power in 1933.

As had happened six years earlier in Germany, Jews in Slovakia lost their rights as citizens. They were dismissed from their jobs in the government, the military, and many other professions. Their businesses were boycotted and forced to close. They were banned from attending schools and from marrying non-Jews. In addition, every Jew was required to wear a yellow armband etched with a black six-pointed Star of David, a traditional symbol of the Jewish people.

In March 1942, authorities began to deport the Jews of Slovakia. *Hlinka* Guards—similar to the uniformed *Schutzstaffel*, or SS, of Nazi Germany—marched entire families to the railroad stations. They crammed their victims into wooden cattle cars without food or water and gave them only a bucket to serve as a toilet. The Jews were allowed, however, to bring along suitcases with their belongings. The guards told the deportees that they would be resettling in Poland, where they would form new communities.

Discrimination against Jews became widespread after Hitler came to power in Germany, requiring them to wear the six-pointed Star of David.

Of the 135,000 Jews who lived in Slovakia in 1939, only about 25,000 would survive the war. More than 80 percent would perish in the ways that Vrba and Wetzler witnessed during their two years at Auschwitz.

As Vrba and Wetzler dwelled on their upcoming plan for escape, they could not help thinking of fellow prisoners who had failed in their own attempts to flee. Vrba had been in Auschwitz for only seven days when two Polish prisoners with civilian clothes in their possession had been caught making plans to escape. The sound of drum rolls had summoned all the camp inmates to witness the hangings of the victims on a pair of portable gallows.

Gallows were used to hang inmates who tried to escape from Auschwitz; after the war, Rudolf Hoess, the camp commandant, was hanged from this structure.

A *kapo*—a prisoner charged with duties overseen by the SS—bound the first man and adjusted the noose around his neck. At the pull of a lever, the platform on which he stood crashed open. But the drop was not deep enough to snap his neck and cause instant death. Slowly, as he gasped for air, the would-be escapee was strangled to death. His accomplice died the same way. Camp officers forced the witnesses to the hangings to remain in their places, with their eyes trained on the dangling bodies, for one hour.

In January 1944, a fellow Slovak prisoner confided in Vrba and Wetzler his foolproof plan to escape from Auschwitz. He had discovered that one of the SS men who had been guarding him happened to be an old schoolmate who had grown up in Slovakia but later had moved to Germany and become outwardly loyal to the Nazi cause.

According to his escape plan, the Slovakian and four other prisoners were simply going to be driven out of the camp with permits obtained by their SS friend. All of them, including the defecting SS man, would then cross the border to freedom.

At the appointed time, the five prisoners approached the place of assembly where the escape vehicle awaited them. They were greeted with blasts of fire. Officers put the escapees' bodies on display inside the camp. Dumdum bullets had torn open their flesh, and their faces and bodies were horribly disfigured. As for their SS "benefactor," his superiors gave him high praise—and a promotion.

Vrba and Wetzler had seen the results of foolishly putting trust in others—especially German officers. Even kapos, the higher-ranking prisoners who did the officers' jobs and dirty work, could not be trusted. So they had decided not to rely on anyone but each other. They would hide in their pile of planks for three days and then make their getaway.

Why three days? At Auschwitz, the search for a missing prisoner or prisoners lasted for three days before it was called off. On the first evening after crawling into their dugout, Vrba and Wetzler could think of nothing but the daily roll call—when their captors would discover them missing—and, following that, the wail of the siren announcing their absence.

That first night, the waiting was almost unbearable. With the first screeching, sickening note of the siren, they would not just become wanted men; they would very possibly become dead men. For, if their plan failed, their only way out of Auschwitz was through the crematorium chimneys.

Vrba and Wetzler could hear the everyday sounds of the camp all around them. Now the officers were marching the prisoners back to their barracks after their daily labors. Orders were shouted. The fierce dogs of the SS yelped and bayed. The thud of rifle butts and the lash of whips hurried the slow, overworked, starvation-weakened prisoners on their way.

From that first day, Vrba and Wetzler knew that any sounds they made within the hideout could give them away. So they had tied flannel cloths around their mouths to stifle the noises of coughs. They had removed the sturdy boots they had managed to acquire and put heavy socks on their feet. (Sitting in cramped positions for days in boots would cause their feet to swell, and they would be unable to run when the time came.) Determined to take their own lives as quickly as possible if they were apprehended, they had armed themselves with razors. Vrba and Wetzler also had some food and water.

It was 5:30! They could tell because they had phosphorescent watches. Roll call had surely taken place by now. When would the siren go off? When would their battle for freedom start? Promptly at 6:00, the thin, bloodcurdling screaming, turned to its fullest volume, began. It could be heard for more than a 10-mile (16-kilometer) radius around the camp. The blast continued for ten minutes.

Soon a thousand or more SS men poured out of their barracks to begin the search. The dogs barked and yelped frenetically as their masters dragged them about to pick up human scents in suspected hideouts. Vrba and Wetzler had thought of the dogs, too. To prevent them from detecting the presence of humans, they had distributed Russian tobacco soaked with gasoline and oil throughout the pile of planks, as well as on themselves. They had learned this trick from Russian prisoners of war at the camp.

The SS men took the dogs off their leashes and had them climb the pile of wood. Vrba and Wetzler could hear claws scrabbling above them. Sawdust and other debris filtered

Large, powerful dogs were trained by their SS masters to catch the scents and to fiercely attack prisoners on command.

down onto their heads. They drew their razors to prepare for quick suicidal slashes to their bodies. Then the dogs pounded their way down to the ground in response to the calls of their owners. No, there didn't seem to be anything in that woodpile.

After what seemed like hours, the noises gradually began to die away. Immediately around the woodpile, it became quiet. Could it be true? Was their first night of raw danger behind them?

By the morning of the second day, Vrba and Wetzler had been in their hideout for seventeen hours. Their bodies were stiff with cold and pain. They dared to stretch a little to relieve their cramped muscles, rigid with fatigue and tension. Could they hold out for close to eighty hours? This was the amount of time it would take for the search to end. Then they would leave their hiding place and make a dash for the outer rim of the camp. Until the search officially ended, armed guards would man the watchtowers that circled the outer cordon of the camp, and there would be no means of escape.

The second and third days of the search for the two missing Slovak Jews were slightly subdued versions of the first. Vrba and Wetzler worried that the gasoline-soaked tobacco would lose its effectiveness against the keen-sniffing dogs. Suppose some of yesterday's SS men returned to the woodpile to conduct a second search. Or what if someone suddenly gave orders to dismantle their hideout for the building of new barracks? How would their bodies respond when the time came to make a run for it, frozen as they were with immobility, the penetrating damp and cold, and lacking nourishment?

At last, it was April 10, 1944, a frosty, foggy Monday morning. Once again the escapees could hear the everyday sounds of the camp—prisoners marching off to work, dogs barking, SS men shouting orders, and the faint strains of the camp orchestra, which was composed of prisoners. The orchestra was intended to rally the energies of the half-starved, near-dying laborers. Many prisoners would not return from their long hours unearthing sand and gravel or raking up the human ashes in the cremation chambers so they could be used as fertilizer.

Vrba and Wetzler could not leave their cramped home of more than three days until after darkness fell. So they spent their time testing their bodies for running. They stretched, bent, flexed, and rotated their arms, legs, and feet. They packed their knapsacks with bread they had been saving for their flight. They put on the boots that would help them run through mud and sand, fields and bracken. Then they waited.

The escapees listened for the sounds of evening. Should they flee at seven o'clock or at eight? Or should they wait until nine? They agreed on nine. The search had been called off for hours. The guard towers of the camp's outer cordon had been vacated.

Finally it was time for Vrba and Wetzler to reach up and start pushing at the timbers above their heads. Outside, a world of new terrors waited for them. But at least it was a world of possibilities—possibilities of freedom and of the chance to reveal the secret of the killing factory of Auschwitz. And it was a chance to try to save those who were slated to be its next victims.

Adolf Hitler rallies the crowds with the Nazi salute in the city of Nuremberg, during the early 1930s, just before seizing power over Germany.

WHEN HITLER BECAME DICTATOR

On March 21, 1933—eleven years before Vrba and Wetzler were about to attempt their escape from Auschwitz—the following headline appeared in the *New York Times*:

REICHSTAG MEETING TODAY IS PREPARED TO GIVE HITLER FULL CONTROL AS DICTATOR.

This was threatening news for the 550,000 Jews living in Germany. Since the end of World War I in 1918, Germany, as a defeated nation, had suffered from severe poverty and a loss of world prestige. As a result of the Treaty of Versailles, which the victorious nations forced the fallen nation to sign, Germany's army was almost completely destroyed, and its economy lay in ruins. A deep-rooted anti-Semitism—prejudice against Jews—sprang to the surface.

Since ancient times, when Jews had been driven from their biblical homeland, they had been a scattered people, dwelling in many different parts of the world, often restricted in their rights and privileges as compared to the nation's citizens.

WHO WAS ADOLF HITLER?

Adolf Hitler was born in an Austrian inn on the German border in 1889. His parents were a minor Austrian customs official and a housekeeper who was roughly half her husband's age. A failing student, Hitler disliked his teachers, refused to study or to submit to discipline, and did not graduate from high school. In *Mein Kampf (My Struggle)*, Hitler's 782-page Nazi bible, he refers to his teachers as "slightly mad," "abnormal," "congenital idiot[s]," and "tyrants."

Eighteen-year-old Hitler's dream was to become an artist. He did not want to be a civil servant as his father demanded. But his efforts to earn entry to the Vienna Academy of Fine Arts proved fruitless. His test drawings were rated as unsatisfactory, and he was advised to study architecture, an unlikely undertaking unless he went back to high school and received his diploma. Hitler then spent several years of poverty in Vienna, where the would-be artist attempted to live by selling postcards of his architectural drawings. When World War I began in 1914, Hitler fought for Germany and was decorated twice. He joined the Nazi Party and rose to become its leader.

The *Reichstag*, or German parliament, appointed Hitler chancellor of Germany in 1933. This role was equivalent to that of a prime minister. It gave him more power than the then-aging German president, whom he would soon supplant as head of state. Under Hitler's leadership, anti-Semitic activities—robbing Jews of their civil rights, their livelihoods, their freedoms, and their safety as citizens—began at once and became increasingly severe.

As part of his effort to expand Germany's territory, Hitler invaded Poland in September 1939. This act led directly to the outbreak of World War II. The Nazis soon began conquests of other European nations. These conquests included herding local Jewish populations into concentration camps to be worked to death or immediately slain.

It took six years, from 1939 to 1945, for the tide of war to turn against the German dictator. On April 30, 1945, Hitler became trapped in an underground bunker in the German capital city of Berlin. To avoid capture by the invading Russian forces, the man who had been responsible for the deaths of at least 11 million civilians (6 million of them Jews) shot himself in the mouth with a revolver.

As the leader of the National Socialist, or Nazi, Party, Adolf Hitler promised Germany newfound glory. He claimed he would restore the honor of his nation's "pure" Aryan (non-Jewish) "master race." Partly at the expense of its middle-class and wealthy Jews, Germany would rearm, rebuild its industries, and even expand its territory.

During Hitler's first year in power, concentration camps began to spring up all over Germany. By the end of 1933, there were at least fifty such camps. Nazi leaders imprisoned not only Jews, but also anti-Nazi activists, German citizens who were deemed to be mentally or physically deficient, Gypsies, and members of the clergy who opposed Hitler. SS men beat and whipped the prisoners and forced them into hard labor. In those early years, however, it was sometimes possible for a prisoner to obtain release, especially if someone paid a ransom on his or her behalf.

As time went on, most Aryan Germans appeared increasingly supportive of the Nazi Party and Hitler's verbal attacks on the Jewish population. Nazi parades, youth marches, and giant demonstrations fanned citizens' patriotism. After Hitler occupied neighboring Austria in 1938, and then Czechoslovakia and Poland in 1939, the Nazis opened a network of concentration camps in the countries to the east. By 1944, along with various subcamps that fed slave laborers into adjacent mines and factories, there were over a thousand camps. Auschwitz—from the German name for the nearby Polish town of Oswiecim—became the largest of the concentration camps.

Built before the Nazi occupation as quarters for the Polish army, the Auschwitz of 1940 was superior in appearance to other camps, which had been built on muddy sites cleared for the purpose of setting up wooden barracks, electrified wire fences, and guard towers. Auschwitz had paved streets and brick buildings. Above the entrance to the camp, the Nazi rulers of occupied Poland had placed an arched metal sign with this puzzling message: *Arbeit Macht Frei* ("Work Brings Freedom").

Vrba and Wetzler describe their first experience of Auschwitz in 1942 as follows:

> After a walk of about 20 minutes with our heavy packs, we reached the concentration camp of Auschwitz. We were at once led into a huge barrack where on the one side we had to deposit all our luggage and on the other side completely undress and leave our valuables behind. Naked, we then proceeded to an adjoining barrack where our heads and bodies were shaved and disinfected with Lysol.

In a third barrack, new prisoners were tattooed with an indelible number that would mark them all their lives as prisoners of Adolf Hitler. The tattoo was located either on the

ARBEIT MACHT FREI ("Work Brings Freedom") was the message first seen by the prisoners of the Nazi labor and extermination camp of Auschwitz.

chest below the collarbone or on the left inner forearm. The rough stamping with sharp metal numbers dipped in Chinese ink caused many prisoners to faint.

In yet another barrack, the newcomers were issued striped prisoners' clothes and ill-fitting wooden clogs that caused blisters and foot deformities. Jewish prisoners were identified with a yellow Star of David, worn as a patch or on an armband. Others had to wear colored triangles indicating the reason for their imprisonment: red for political prisoners, pink for homosexuals, green for professional criminals, black for Russian prisoners of war, and violet for members of religious sects that protested Nazism. Polish prisoners, of whom there were a great many, had a letter P in the middle of their triangles.

On the separate days of their arrival at Auschwitz, Vrba and Wetzler discovered that they were not going to live in the brick buildings they had first encountered. After guards marched them some 2.5 miles (4 km), they came upon the muddy, desolate grounds of an adjacent camp that was still being built in a former birch forest. This camp would be known

Prisoners were tattooed with a number, issued striped uniforms, and meticulously photographed to preserve their identities, upon arrival at Auschwitz.

by three names: Birkenau, Auschwitz-Birkenau, or Auschwitz II. Within a year, however, it would become part of the great killing complex generally referred to as Auschwitz.

For now, Birkenau was just a raw beginning. Russian prisoners had built its few stone barracks. Many of them had died of overwork and starvation, and their bodies lay not far away in shallow ground, giving off the appalling smell of death.

Vrba and Wetzler lived in the three-tiered bunks of the barracks—three people to a bunk—with five hundred other prisoners. They ate thin turnip soup for lunch and bread and tea for supper. On rare occasions, there would be a cube of potato in the soup. The bread contained sawdust; the tea was muddy. And their labor assignment was to dig up the rotting corpses of thousands of Russians for reburial in deeper ground or for burning.

Planning for the Final Solution

Prisoners were useful as laborers. They could be put to work building new camps, clearing ground, and hauling materials. They could be forced to labor in factories, producing war materials and synthetic rubber. And yet, the success of their persecution of the Jews in Europe created problems for the Nazi hierarchy. When the able-bodied prisoners died, they could be replaced with new waves of workers—but there were still too many of them for burial. And how were the camps to dispose of those who were too young or too frail to be useful?

On January 20, 1942, fifteen high officials of the Nazi government met in the Berlin suburb of Wannsee to clear up the fundamental problems of what came to be popularly known in Germany as the "Final Solution to the Jewish Question." Although the Jews of Germany itself had been whittled down to only 130,000 by this time, there were still millions in Poland, Russia, the remains of central Europe, France, and England, which Hitler planned to invade.

Newly-arrived, able-bodied women prisoners from Russia, who have been selected for forced labor, stand at roll call.

A direct result of the Wannsee Conference took place on July 17, 1942, when Heinrich Himmler, the leader of the SS, made an official visit to Auschwitz. With great pomp and ceremony, camp commander Rudolf Hoess showed Himmler both the accomplishments and the defects of the camp. Hoess reported that the bespectacled, almost meek-looking Himmler coolly "watched the whole process of destruction of a transport of Jews, which had just arrived. He also spent a short time watching the selection of the able-bodied Jews."

Hoess pointed out the deficiencies of Auschwitz—"the overcrowded huts and the primitive and insufficient latrines and wash houses . . . the high rate of sickness and death." But Himmler showed little interest in the cramped and miserable lives of the prisoners. Of concern to him were, as Vrba quotes,

> the grossly inefficient methods which were being used to exterminate the Jews who were beginning to arrive in their thousands from all parts of Europe.
>
> The gas chambers were no more than makeshift affairs. The burning of the bodies in open trenches wasted valuable fuel and caused the Germans who by that time occupied the nearby Polish town of Auschwitz to complain of the stench. . . .
>
> And so he gave orders for the greatest, most efficient extermination factory that the world has ever known.

In January 1943, Himmler returned for a second visit to Auschwitz, this time to observe the workings of the newly-built crematoria at Birkenau, the plans for which had gone into effect seven months earlier. Conveyor-belt killing would now be the order of the day. Tracks connected the gas chamber to the fifteen ovens, each capable of burning three bodies at a time in about twenty minutes.

The process went as follows: The victims who had been selected for extermination (selections were usually made on Mondays and Thursdays) were told to undress for the purpose of taking a shower. To prevent panic among those who suspected the lie, guards often gave the prisoners a towel and a small piece of soap. They then crowded the prisoners into the large chamber, body to body, so that there was barely room to stand. The doors were shut and sealed.

After a short interval during which the temperature rose in the chamber, the SS officer called up to the roof to order the kapos, who were wearing gas masks, to open the traps and release pellets of Zyklon B, a cyanide compound that turns into a deadly gas at a given temperature. Within as little as three minutes, all the victims in the chamber were dead.

Camp workers opened, aired, and cleaned the chamber. The bodies were carted in flat trucks along tracks to the crematorium furnaces. Before the bodies were burned, however, a "special squad" of prisoners had to extract gold teeth from the mouths of the corpses, cut the women's hair to be used for making cloth, and search body parts for concealed diamonds or other jewelry.

So great was the "success" of the new gassing and crematorium factory at Auschwitz-Birkenau that, as Vrba and Wetzler later reported, "Prominent guests from

Two of the fifteen crematorium furnaces at Auschwitz, in which the bodies of gas-chamber victims could rapidly be burned.

A gas chamber at Auschwitz, into which prisoners were tightly packed and died within minutes from the fumes of Zyklon B

Berlin were present at the inauguration in March 1943. The 'program' consisted of the gassing and burning of 8,000 Cracow [Polish] Jews. The guests, both officers and civilians, were extremely satisfied with the results and the special peephole fitted into the door of the gas chamber was in constant use. They were lavish in their praise of this newly erected installation."

How Did the United States React to Hitler Germany?

NAZIS SMASH, LOOT AND BURN JEWISH SHOPS AND TEMPLES . . . This was the headline in the *New York Times* of November 11, 1938. The article read, "A wave of destruction, looting and incendiarism unparalleled in Germany since the Thirty Years War . . . swept over Great Germany today as National Socialist cohorts took vengeance on Jewish shops, offices and synagogues for the murder by a young Polish Jew of Ernst von Rath, third secretary of the German Embassy in Paris."

Starting on November 9 and continuing through November 10, almost every town and city in Germany and Austria rang with the sound of broken glass from the smashed windows of Jewish-owned shops. Furniture and even pianos from the homes of Jewish inhabitants thudded to the ground and were hacked to pieces by mobs gone wild. Huge fires gutted synagogues, Jewish orphanages and hospitals, and other Jewish-owned properties. The SS took between 20,000 and 30,000 Jews, mainly men, from their homes, arrested them, and placed them in concentration camps.

This fierce and open assault on Jews came to be known as *Kristallnacht*, or the "Night of Broken Glass." The world reaction was one of shock and dismay. How could a centuries-old Christian nation—the home of some of the world's greatest composers, writers, thinkers, and scientists—behave with such barbarity?

On November 14, 1938, President Franklin Roosevelt recalled the American ambassador to Germany and, on November 18, Hitler recalled the German ambassador to the United States. The Nazi dictator was furious with the expressions of condemnation that he received from abroad. He exclaimed that his critics were all members of "the Jewish world conspiracy."

The windows of Jewish-owned shops were smashed in the Nazi assault on Jews and their property known as *Kristallnacht*.

But how far was the United States prepared to go to help the doomed Jewish populations of Europe? Between 1933 and 1945, Hitler's years as dictator, only a small fraction of the 6 million who were put to death was allowed to obtain refuge in the United States. This happened because the immigration quotas allotted to citizens of foreign countries were limited—and they remained so in spite of the ongoing slaughter abroad. It happened because of ingrained American isolationism and anti-Semitism that operated even within the liberal Roosevelt administration. It happened in spite of warnings, pleas, and proof of the mounting exterminations in Nazi-dominated Europe.

Beginning in 1939, with the war going on, few messengers could report on what was happening in Europe. Nonetheless, an underground Polish organization known as the Jewish Labor Bund described mass killings in Poland. This report became public on the BBC in London in June 1942.

In summer 1941, the Jewish Labor Bund reported, "men, fourteen to sixty years old, were driven to a single place . . . where they were slaughtered or shot by machine guns or killed by hand grenades. They had to dig their own graves. Children in orphanages, inmates in old-age homes, the sick in hospitals were shot, women were killed in the streets."

Until they built gas chambers in many of the concentration camps, the Nazis employed mobile gas vans in Poland. They crammed in as many as ninety people at a time and murdered up to one thousand a day. In June 1942, the London *Daily Telegraph* headlined the fact that 700,000 Polish Jews had been exterminated in this fashion. The *New York Times* had received the same information but buried the report in its back pages.

As the war raged on and concentration camps were equipped with gas chambers and crematoria, especially those at

Auschwitz-Birkenau, Jewish organizations and governments-in-exile, such as that of Poland, begged the U.S. and British air forces to bomb the rail lines leading to the death camps. The two nations, however, responded that they did not have sufficient aircraft for the purpose. President Franklin Roosevelt further stated that the objective was first to win the war and then to rescue its civilian victims.

Thus, in 1944, Vrba and Wetzler found themselves on the lip of a daring attempt to escape. In their small way, they hoped to take a huge step toward alerting the world to the operation of the Auschwitz killing ground.

Prisoners assigned to forced labor worked long hours and were severely punished for inefficiency or for damage to tools or work materials.

THE AUSCHWITZ-BIRKENAU DEATH FACTORY

During his time at Auschwitz, Rudolf Vrba received a variety of labor assignments. His first job was in the vast Buna chemical plant, "to which we were herded every morning at about 3 a.m. The way to and from work had to be covered at a brisk military trot; anyone falling out of line was shot. Very few could bear the strain and although escape seemed hopeless, attempts were made every day. The result was several hangings a week."

Weeks of painful and exhausting work ended for Vrba when a typhus epidemic broke out at the plant. Hundreds of the three thousand or so prisoner-laborers died, while survivors were sent to the gravel pit, where the work was even more strenuous. Vrba and others contracted swollen feet. Camp officers selected those unable to work and sent them to Birkenau to be gassed.

Vrba, hearing that there was an opening in the so-called "clearing squad," made an application. Because he spoke German as well as Polish and his native Slovak tongue, he was accepted. Through his new job, Vrba learned of the enormous economic benefits that Nazi Germany was deriving from the stolen possessions of its victims.

In a far corner of the camp that was nicknamed Canada because of its wealth, Vrba reported, "we found huge sheds full of knapsacks, suitcases, and other luggage. We had to open each piece of baggage and sort the contents into large cases specially prepared for each category of goods."

Innocently believing that they were being deported for the purpose of forming new communities, the Nazis' victims had packed both necessities and valuables for their journey. But, after arriving at the ramp from which they exited

Female prisoners at Auschwitz sort through the shoes of murdered Hungarian Jews in the clearing warehouse known as Canada.

the railroad cars and entered the concentration camp, the prisoners never saw their luggage again. At Auschwitz, Vrba reported, he and his fellow prisoners sorted goods ranging from combs, mirrors, and medicines to canned food, sugar, chocolate, and kitchenware. Clothing, furs, and blankets were a special category that prisoners had to sort according to their condition and value. Most highly prized were gold, cash, jewelry, and precious stones found among the belongings of the deceived travelers.

Working in the clearing squad, although physically easier than laboring at Buna or in the gravel pit, had its own hazards. The slightest suspicion that one of the sorters had taken a valuable article could lead to instant punishment by flogging or even death. Prisoners had to turn over gold, gems, and money to the camp authorities. Clothing was shipped back to Germany, where some was distributed to the families of German soldiers. Fur coats were remodeled into garments for troops battling the Soviet Union on the frigid eastern front.

Workers stripped the newly arrived prisoners of their eyeglasses, artificial teeth and limbs, walking canes, baby carriages, and even hair soon after they entered the camp. These items, too, were sent to Germany, where they had many uses. Nothing was wasted. The clearing squad even had to squeeze the toothpaste out of prisoners' tubes in case the deportees had hidden diamonds or other stones in the paste. The only items of little interest to the Nazi authorities were documents and family portraits. These mementos of lost lives saddened Vrba.

Despite his efforts to do his job honestly, Vrba was soon caught in a web of petty favoritism. The kapo who directly supervised him persuaded him to take a small gift to a female kapo. The SS officer in charge apprehended Vrba and his kapo. Following a severe beating on his legs, Vrba was sent to the camp hospital, from which many patients were selected for the gas chamber. His youth, along with the better diet given to members of the clearing squad, probably saved his life. Vrba survived the surgery that was necessary to relieve his swelling, and camp leaders reassigned him. He took up his new position on the platform at the base of the ramp where railroad cars emptied their human cargoes into the Auschwitz-Birkenau camp. Meanwhile, the guilty kapo lost not only his position of trust, but also his life.

Vrba's eight months of working on the platform, where he witnessed the selection process of hundreds of transports, confirmed his decision to escape Auschwitz by any means possible and to inform the world of its evil. It was during this period that he ran into Fred Wetzler, someone he had admired but never spoken to back in his hometown in Slovakia. The two countrymen instantly agreed on their goal of escape. Wetzler, too, had experienced and witnessed the brutalities that Auschwitz prisoners were suffering hour upon hour.

Wetzler's initial assignment at Auschwitz-Birkenau involved the reburial of corpses. The SS men had buried the bodies of about eight thousand Russian prisoners of war—who

Jewish women and children, having just descended from the railway cattle cars at Auschwitz, await the fearful process of selection.

SS officers at Auschwitz took advantage of their authority by confiscating the jewelry and other valuables of the prisoners brought there to die.

had died of wounds, disease, or starvation—in the shallow, muddy flats of Birkenau before the crematoria were built. Under the scrutiny of the SS command, Wetzler and his fellow laborers descended into the swamp from which sticklike arms and legs protruded. They lifted the partially decomposed bodies onto small trucks, wheeled them to a large trench, and emptied them into yet another mass grave.

After the crematoria were finished, Wetzler worked as the registrar at the camp morgue. The building consisted of a large, wooden barrack where the bodies of the dead were stacked before cremation. It was Wetzler's job to record the numbers tattooed on the prisoners' inner forearms so that they could be checked against the information on their entry cards. Wetzler was also responsible for turning over the gold teeth of the corpses to the SS. The extractions were the job of four Polish prisoners, armed with pliers and a tin can.

Sometimes the morgue was full and bodies had to be stacked 6 feet (1.8 meters) high, with yet others lying at the back of the building. Other times there were as few as forty victims. The number of bodies awaiting cremation depended on how many prisoners had died in the night in their bunks, how many had dropped in their tracks at work, and how high the day's punishment rate had been.

Wetzler's everyday contact with corpses was a tormenting reminder of his own family's unknown fate. In 1942, before he was put on the transport from Slovakia to Poland, his two older brothers and his father had been deported. He believed that they, too, had been taken to Auschwitz. He could only guess that they were no longer alive.

Both Vrba and Wetzler recorded the struggles and hazards that they and their fellow prisoners faced while living at Auschwitz. From reveille at four o'clock in the morning to the distribution of bread for the evening meal, their everyday lives were plagued with cold and hunger, pain and disease, overwork, and the threat of punishment for the slightest infraction. Latrines were filthy and lacked privacy. Water for washing was scarce. Malaria, typhus, and dysentery raged through the barracks. The emaciated and the very sick stumbled through their days until they dropped of natural causes or the SS singled them out for extermination.

Wetzler wrote of the "trembling hands" of the prisoners as they reached out for their portion of bread each evening. Everyone hoped for an entire piece with all of its crust intact. Some ate their bread immediately; others hid their treasures under their straw mattresses to eat in the morning—after guarding it carefully through the night. Crumbs that fell to the ground immediately disappeared into someone's mouth. If prisoners died in the night, their bunkmates searched their pockets and mattresses for a hidden prize.

Vrba wrote about the camp's routines on days of Christian observance such as Sundays and Christmas. In deference to the Lutheran religion that most Germans practiced, Sunday was a so-called day of rest. The inmates did not have to go to work. It was forbidden to hold Sunday religious services in the camp, however—not even Lutheran services. Polish priests who tried to conduct Catholic Masses were put to death. Jews, who made up most of the camp's population, observed their Sabbath on Friday nights and Saturdays. Jews who prayed took every precaution to do so in secret.

Sundays at Auschwitz were also the time for meticulous inspections of the barracks and for "physical culture" exercises. Just in case the idleness of the day rendered the prisoners lazy and flabby, they had to line up for stretching and bending drills, running in place, and other Hitlerian "Health-Through-Joy" routines.

The Nazi overseers of the camp often grew sentimental about Christmas and about their families at home. This was a dangerous time of year for the Jewish prisoners, for their ancient forebears had been accused of bringing about the crucifixion of Jesus Christ. As a relatively mild form of punishment, Nazis ordered every barrack to sing "Silent Night" on Christmas Eve.

The meeting of Vrba and Wetzler took place sometime in autumn 1943. They had been working near each other for some time. Vrba began to spend whatever time he could manage at the mortuary with Wetzler. The two soon held serious discussions to devise an infallible escape plan. A series of deceptive and murderous events at Auschwitz between September 1943 and March 1944 helped hold them fast to their decision. These events began with the shipment of some seven thousand Czech Jews to Auschwitz from the camp known as Theresienstadt, in Czechoslovakia.

On a snowy day in March 1944, Vrba and Wetzler explored an area of the camp where building materials for future barracks were stacked. Most were in uniform piles of either doorframes or wall units. The piles were compact and contained no spaces within.

THE NAZI DECEPTION OF THE THERESIEN- STADT JEWS

The camp known as Theresienstadt, in German, or Terezin, in Czech, existed from November 1941 to May 1945. Unlike other Nazi concentration camps, Theresienstadt was said to be a "model" camp—more of a "privileged" ghetto than a forced-labor or killing center. Jews from Germany, Austria, and Czechoslovakia were allowed to live there in family groups. They wore their own clothing and directed some of their own community activities. Children attended school.

Space was limited, however, and from time to time groups of Theresienstadt Jews were moved to killing centers. According to the Vrba-Wetzler report, "During the week following September 7, 1943, family transports of Jews arrived from Theresienstadt." At first, camp authorities permitted the more than four thousand new arrivals to continue living as families. No one shaved their heads, they kept their luggage and wore their own clothing, and "[they] were lodged in a separate section of the camp, men, women and children together."

As the months of the so-called "quarantine" of the Theresienstadt Jews passed, Vrba and Wetzler kept a watchful eye on the group. They made contact with its leader and encouraged him to organize an uprising, in which the rest of the camp would join if the authorities threatened to strip them of their privileges and gas them. In the meantime, on December 20, 1943, another group of three thousand Jews arrived from Theresienstadt. Initially, they had the same privileges in Auschwitz as the earlier arrivals.

On March 6, 1944, Vrba and Wetzler learned that camp workers were preparing the crematoria for the first contingent of Theresienstadt Jews. The pair immediately informed the leader of the Czech Jews. When the Auschwitz prison system told him that he could do nothing to save his people, he took poison. The following day, SS men rounded up his comrades and delivered them to the gas chambers.

Vrba and Wetzler reported, "Of all these Jews only 11 twins were left alive. They are being subjected to various medical tests at Auschwitz. A week before the gassing, that is to say on March 1, 1944, everyone in the Czech camp had been asked to inform his relatives about his well-being. The letters had to be dated March 23 to 25, 1944, and they were requested to ask for food parcels."

One pile was different, however. It was composed of mixed hut sections that were stacked more loosely, and it had an interior space accessible via a short passageway. Upon entering the passageway on his belly, Vrba discovered a shallow trench. There was just enough room for him and Wetzler.

Soon, with the help of trusty comrades, Vrba and Wetzler began to supply their three-day hideout with heavy socks and warm clothing, vitamins and glucose tablets, a cigarette lighter, and a flashlight. Those who strongly supported the message that Vrba and Wetzler planned to take to the outside world had managed to obtain these items at great peril. As evidence of their knowledge of Auschwitz, Vrba and Wetzler also would carry diagrams of the camp layout (including the crematoria), transport lists, names of brutal SS officers, and a label from a canister of Zyklon B.

At last, the entry into the hideout was only days away. "If anything comes up," Wetzler told Vrba, "or if anything is needed, I'll let you know. And if we don't see each other, or if I've been unable to send word to you, then on Friday. . . . Go now and be very careful!"

Entrance to the Auschwitz-Birkenau death camp. Today this prison has been turned into a state museum in Ocwiecim, Poland.

ESCAPE INTO THE UNKNOWN

It was time: Monday, April 10, 1944, at about nine o'clock on the evening of a chilly spring day. The night sky was clear, and there was a slight ground mist. Fortunately for Vrba and Wetzler, there had been no snow to leave telltale signs as they crawled to the perimeter of the camp.

At first, the escapees' bodies were cramped and weak. Their arms were so stiff that they could not lift and separate the wooden planks that sheltered them. It was as if the panels had frozen into a solid mass, trapping them permanently in what was to have been a temporary hideout. Time and again they reached above their heads, only to sink to their knees.

So far, the two had lived solely on water, as they were saving their bread for the nights of running and days of hiding that lay ahead of them. They broke into a sweat and struggled to catch their breath. Finally, after repeated tries, they pried the first panel loose. Others gave way. When at last Vrba and

Wetzler emerged into the night air, they had a momentary, deceptive sense of having been liberated.

But they knew they were a long way from freedom. The sight of the belching crematoria chimneys reminded them of the dangers that lay all around them. Long searchlight beams illuminated the main roads of the camp and the passageways between the barracks. Lights twinkled from the pylons that marked the barbed wire fence surrounding the camp.

Vrba and Wetzler's escape route lay to the south, roughly 80 miles (130 km) through Nazi-occupied Poland to the border with Slovakia. Wearing their boots and Dutch-made woolen civilian suits—obtained at great risk by clearing-squad friends—and dragging a heavy rucksack of warm socks and underwear behind them, their first challenge was to wriggle beneath the wire fence strung around the perimeter of the camp.

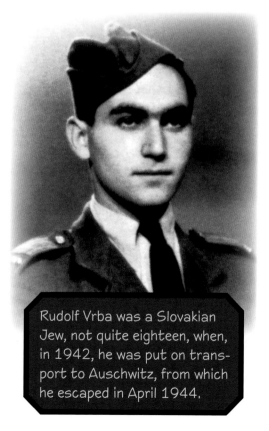

Rudolf Vrba was a Slovakian Jew, not quite eighteen, when, in 1942, he was put on transport to Auschwitz, from which he escaped in April 1944.

Alfred Wetzler, Vrba's countryman and fellow-escapee, was in his mid-twenties when he arrived in Auschwitz, where he became the morgue registrar.

A ditch conveniently ran beneath the fence for a short distance. It was deep enough to allow Vrba and Wetzler to raise the bottom wires and hold them in place while each man slid through. Crawling on their elbows and knees, as close to the ground as possible, Vrba and Wetzler let themselves down into the ditch. They propped the bottom wires with wooden pegs they had brought with them and with flat stones from the field.

Hauling up the heavy rucksack was difficult. But Vrba and Wetzler dared not think of abandoning it. The sack was direct evidence of their escape. If SS men found it, it would be a death sentence that would usher them back to Auschwitz and its smoking chimneys.

Nor did safety lie ahead. Along the two young men's route lay satellite slave-labor camps that served as subdivisions of Auschwitz. Also, since the Nazi occupation, German peasants had taken over the countryside, which had once been dotted with Polish farmhouses. The German farmers had orders to shoot on sight any strangers passing through their land or in the nearby forests.

Upon reaching the first small wooded area, Vrba and Wetzler could go no further. Their knees and elbows stung with the pain of crawling along flat, open terrain. Exhausted, they fell to the ground, opened their rucksack, and made a banquet of a rationed portion of the bread they had saved for this moment. It was the first food they had eaten in ninety-two hours.

In the Line of German Fire

Six days passed. Vrba and Wetzler ran by night and slept by day in sheltered areas, where they hoped to remain hidden. They drank water from streams, and they quickly finished the last of their bread. Hunger, fatigue, and fear of detection became their constant companions.

As escaping prisoners they knew they were ready targets, not only of German farmers but also of Nazi military outposts planted throughout occupied Poland. Moving only by night, they often lost their way and found themselves dangerously close to settled areas or even small towns in the morning. One day at dawn, they stepped out of the forest atop a small hill and looked down on a lake with a hydropower station. The dam was protected with barrage balloons and guarded by a German regiment housed in two long military barracks. The hillsides above the power station were bare, devoid of even the slightest hint of cover.

Vrba cursed. There had been so many desperate nights of stumbling in the dark, becoming bloody and sore from scrapes and falls, suffering from painfully swollen feet, yet trying to make haste. Would they ever get far enough away from the Nazi murderers? They could even see the figures of the soldiers moving about below them. When evening came, they would have to be on the run again. But how would they get past the gun sites of the sentinels, who would surely turn on their anti-aircraft searchlights at the slightest sound?

All day the two young men waited. When an early evening gloom enveloped their mountain hideout, they agreed that it was time to make a run for the crest. Yet they had to do so silently. Even the snap of a twig would be audible in the still air. And sure enough, even before the first beams of the searchlights swept the hillside, shots rang out. Vrba and Wetzler froze and clung to the ground. Bullets whizzed directly above their heads. The escapees could hear them pinging against the rocks.

In spite of their bloody feet and emaciated bodies, Vrba and Wetzler ran in the direction of steepest ascent, as a burst of adrenaline vaulted them just beyond the point of danger. Then all was silent. Had they really outrun the German bullets?

Vrba and Wetzler brought a torn label from a canister of deadly Zyklon B cyanide pellets with them to Slovakia to show evidence of the Nazi killings.

Breathing heavily, they lay on the ground facedown. When they finally turned to look behind them, the searchlights were gone. The pinging of the bullets had ceased. Incredibly, by mere chance, neither of them had been hit. At last they sank into a patch of snow in a grove of evergreens. In spite of the cold wind they dampened their foreheads and raw palms with the icy crystals and placed bits of melting snow on their tongues.

Vrba asked Wetzler to cut open his boots and remove them from his swollen feet. The pain of the puffed and broken skin was no longer bearable. Wetzler nodded silently. Gently he wielded one of the razors they had brought. He had to slit the leather from toe to heel to free Vrba's clinging, bloody foot from the boot's embrace. Then he slit open Vrba's other shoe, removed his own boots, and threw both pairs into the bushes. The two men cleaned off the blood with snow and wrapped their bare feet in strips of cloth. Now, Wetzler remarked, let the Germans send their dogs. They might find the boots. But they wouldn't find the feet of a pair of escaping prisoners inside them.

The supplies of the two escaping prisoners had dwindled rapidly. All that remained in their rucksack were their medicines, their razors, their wristwatches, a map, and a flashlight. They also had bits of cloth that once had been socks and underwear but now served to bind their feet and other wounded parts of their bodies. Suddenly Wetzler cried out. The metal tube, which contained detailed ground plans of Auschwitz, was missing. It probably had rolled away when they were running clumsily from German fire and dragging the rucksack behind them.

Vrba assured Wetzler that he could redraw the plans from memory. The other metal tube, which housed lists of the transports and their origins, the numbers of prisoners delivered to Auschwitz, the Zyklon B label, and the names and ranks of the entire SS, was safe.

To Reach Slovakia

It was early evening of another wearying day—the ninth since Vrba and Wetzler's escape from Auschwitz. The two men wondered how long they would be able to hold out against their gnawing hunger. More than once they had been tempted to approach a distant farmhouse and knock on the door. But they knew they were all too likely to end up looking into the barrel of a shotgun.

The two escapees were just leaving a shelter of trees and dense bushes, in which they had concealed themselves during the day, when they were alarmed to see a woman and a boy coming toward them over the brow of the hill. In spite of the dying light, the sharp-eyed woman spotted the tattered, dirt-covered travelers at once. As she approached them straightforwardly, she encouraged the boy not to be afraid of the two young men.

The woman's glance took in Vrba and Wetzler's once-fine woolen suits, smudged with mud and torn by brambles, and their feet wrapped in filthy rags. She questioned them in a friendly manner. Had they come far? Where were they going? Vrba and Wetzler glanced at each other and mumbled something about being on their way to work. The woman smiled knowingly. Perhaps, she suggested, they were on their way to Slovakia on the Polish frontier.

So, she'd guessed that they were runaways. The young men nodded helplessly. The woman talked on and doled out valuable information. The distance to the frontier was not great, she said. But the escapees would have little chance of making it on those feet. And did they know the mountain trails they must follow in order to reach the safest crossing point at the frontier?

Vrba and Wetzler were forced to admit their ignorance. They knew nothing of the dangerous trails that approached the border. Surely Nazi soldiers were patrolling the area. But could they trust this woman? How could they be certain that she was not in the service of Poland's German overlords?

Almost as though she'd read their thoughts, the woman blurted out, "If you really trust me, then wait here until tomorrow. I'll come again at this time—with my brother-in-law. He knows these mountains like the back of his hand, he'll guide you across safely."

Worried about the possibility of falling into a Nazi trap, Vrba and Wetzler watched the woman open the rucksack she'd been carrying. Methodically, she removed old blankets, ordinarily used for gathering firewood, and—to the amazement of the starving men—two small, round loaves of black bread. The blankets, she explained, would protect them from the damp ground and keep them warm through the night. The bread needed no explanation. Famished after days of living only on bitter-tasting, hard, bluish berries and water, the two seized the loaves and, to their embarrassment, began chewing immediately.

No sooner had the woman and boy left than a disagreement broke out. Vrba was still suspicious. Suppose they *were* being set up for capture. Why not move on now while their bellies were full? Why waste another day?

A five-digit tattoo, stamped on the arm of an elderly survivor of Auschwitz, is faded but remains indelible.

Wetzler did not think they were about to be betrayed. He believed that, in spite of all the two had suffered, it was important to learn to trust—to believe that there were still courageous people willing to help others, even at risk to themselves.

Finally the two settled down for the night. Ever watchful, they dozed in shifts. In the morning, they washed in rivulets of melted snow. During the day they nibbled on the hard, blue berries that covered the ground. The berries were not only bitter. They had yellow centers that burned the lips and tongue like hot peppers and seemed to make them hungrier the more they ate. So they switched to eating grass, which they first chewed into a paste.

Just as it seemed that dusk would never fall, the woman and boy came into view. They introduced their companion, a short man with a firm step, as Tadeusz. He wore a cap that partly covered his face, and his first gesture was to approach Wetzler and roughly pull up the left sleeve of the escapee's jacket. There, indelibly stamped on Wetzler's forearm, was his tattooed prisoner number—29162. Tadeusz nodded. It appeared that this was the escapee number he had been expecting. For, along with Vrba's number—44070—it had appeared in the warrant that was out for the former prisoners' arrest.

Tadeusz gave sharp instructions. They would have to make the border crossing that night, for he was a skilled laborer in a German factory and had to be at work in the morning. Tadeusz had carefully concealed his Jewish identity—and his role in the underground—from the Nazis. Along with other brave people, Tadeusz was part of a chain of delivery for escaped prisoners seeking their way through the mountains of southern Poland into Slovakia.

To the delight of Vrba and Wetzler, the woman produced cooked cabbage and potatoes, bread, and goat's milk from

"TELL EVERYONE ABOUT AUSCHWITZ"

The most urgent aspect of Vrba and Wetzler's escape from Auschwitz-Birkenau lay after they reached safety. How, despite the evidence they carried with them, were they going to get officials of the anti-Nazi underground to believe them?

The former prisoners also would have to avoid personal danger, for Slovakia was still a puppet of Nazi Germany, and Vrba and Wetzler bore the tattoos of Auschwitz on their arms. Above all, they had to make effective underground contacts, who would quickly forward their information to powers that might be able to stop the slaughter in the camps. Those powers were primarily England and the United States.

Already, unbeknownst to Vrba and Wetzler, brave individuals had made efforts to bring eyewitness reports directly to the leaders of those nations. As early as 1942, they had pleaded with British and U.S leaders to bomb the rail lines leading to the concentration camps of Europe. But the American president, Franklin Roosevelt, had stated that his first goal was to win the war against Germany. The next operation would be the elimination of the camps. Gruesome reports of mass killings had reached London and New York, but they had been buried in the back pages of newspapers focusing primarily on the major battles of the war.

Vrba and Wetzler also knew of the Nazi plan to round up the last of Europe's major Jewish populations—the 725,000 Jews of Hungary—starting in May 1944. The Nazis would send most of the new prisoners to Auschwitz, where workers were building extra barracks. There, the

"Hungarian salami," as the SS jokingly referred to their incoming transports, would either perform heavy labor assignments or fall victim to the gas chambers and ovens of Auschwitz-Birkenau.

her knapsack The young men hadn't eaten such a meal since they'd left home two years earlier.

"Rags," Tadeusz reminded the woman, when Vrba and Wetzler had eaten the last of the strength-renewing food. "You haven't given them the rags yet."

The soreness of Vrba and Wetzler's swollen and badly lacerated feet would be a hazard if they were to reach the frontier by morning. They would have to scramble in the dark through brambles and thick undergrowth, over sharp rocks, and across mountain streams. So, once again, they wrapped their feet in thick layers of cloth. After hugging the escapees, the woman sent them on their way with Tadeusz. She wished them a happy reunion with their mothers and cautioned them not to drink too much water, lest their feet swell even more.

The night crossing, under the discipline of their Polish guide, was one of breathlessness, sweat, and pain. Barely stopping to look back at his followers, Tadeusz marched on. He allowed a half hour's rest at midnight, after which he commanded the young men to get to their feet and start moving again.

Some hours later, in the early morning darkness, Tadeusz delivered the two escapees to a spot within view of the Slovakian frontier. "When it gets light," he told them, "you'll see the marker posts." He reminded them that the success of the rest of their mission was up to them. Vrba and Wetzler were now little more than a stone's throw from their native land. In gratitude, they embraced Tadeusz, who delivered the final words, "Tell everyone about Auschwitz."

Wachgebäude für K.G.L.

Vorderansicht.

Schnitt c-d

Hinteransicht.

Schnitt e-f

II. Stockgrundriss

Werksatz

Seitenansicht.

A recently discovered portion of a set of plans of the Auschwitz death camp, showing its gas chamber and its crematoria.

THE VRBA-WETZLER REPORT: INTO THE PAGES OF HISTORY

It was the last week of April 1944. The Slovakian Jewish Council had given Vrba and Wetzler a hideout in a nearly deserted elderly people's home in the city of Zilina. To ensure the escapees' safety, they had traveled to their new residence by ambulance. This was the most recent place of refuge that the underground had secured for Vrba and Wetzler. There the pair met with the council's representatives to inform them of what was taking place in Auschwitz and to get word to the Jewish Aid and Rescue Committee in Hungary about the upcoming deportations of the Jews.

But even before Vrba and Wetzler could send their warning to Rudolf Kastner, the well-known leader of the Hungarian

THE HUNGARIAN JEWS BETRAYED

Until March 1944, Nazi Germany had looked upon the small nation of Hungary as an ally. Hungarian military forces had fought alongside Germany during its invasion of the Soviet Union. Due to Hungary's loyalty to Hitler, the nation's 725,000 Jews had been spared deportation thus far. In fact, a Hungarian Jewish lawyer named Rudolf Kastner was on such amicable terms with German officials that he had established the Aid and Rescue Committee to offer sanctuary in Hungary to Jews from elsewhere in Europe.

Hungary's status as a more or less free state changed abruptly when Germany discovered that the Hungarian government was secretly negotiating with the United States and Great Britain in an attempt to shift sides in the war. In March 1944, Nazi Germany occupied Hungary and put its high-ranking Gestapo official, Adolf Eichmann, in charge of deporting the nation's Jews.

As Kastner had been on friendly terms with Eichmann, many people hoped that the popular Jewish leader, who had rescued Jews in the past, would somehow save the Jews of Hungary. Even if Eichmann turned his back on Kastner, Jewish underground leaders—along with Vrba and Wetzler—were counting on Kastner to publicly proclaim the truth about the camps. If Kastner informed his people that they were about to be sent to death factories rather than "resettlement" sites, a massive rebellion against deportation might take place.

When the time came, however, Kastner made no move to stop the deportation of some 450,000 Hungarian Jews to Auschwitz. Between May and July 1944, roughly 12,000 people per day were dispatched to Poland.

It was during that period that the scandal regarding the "Kastner train" came to light. On June 30, 1944, a train carrying 1,684 wealthy Jews, family members, and other privileged people left the Hungarian capital city of Budapest for neutral Switzerland. How had this come about at a time when hundreds of thousands of Jews were being sent to their deaths? In a deal that Kastner had made with Eichmann, the passengers had paid for their freedom with money, gold, and diamonds.

After the war ended—and after 550,000 Hungarian Jews had been murdered in the death camps—Kastner moved to Israel. There, the question of his guilt in arranging for the "Kastner train" became a serious issue. In 1954, he went on trial and was convicted of collaboration with the Nazis. On March 15, 1957, Kastner died of wounds resulting from an assassination attempt near his home in Tel Aviv.

Eichmann fled to Argentina after the war. He lived there under a false identity until the Mossad, Israel's secret service, captured him in 1960. Eichmann went to trial in Israel, where he was executed by hanging in 1962.

Jews, they discovered that they were too late. The escapees had been at their new quarters only a short time when they learned that thousands of Hungarian deportees were already being shipped to Auschwitz in cattle cars. The railroad wagons carrying the new prisoners to their deaths were, in fact, passing directly through Zilina on their way to Poland.

The two young men were despondent. They had had so much hope that Kastner, who had been able to save many Jews from the camps in the past, would be able to save the vast majority. Had there been a failure of communication or an outright betrayal?

Three Days to Write a Report

The news of the first deportations of the Hungarian Jews made Vrba and Wetzler more anxious than ever to report the details of their captivity in Auschwitz to their Jewish underground contacts. They hoped those contacts would spread the word to both anti-Nazi and neutral officials worldwide, to religious authorities such as the pope in Rome, and to humanitarian organizations such as the International Red Cross.

But even in their earliest interview sessions, Vrba and Wetlzer saw that the underground representatives—a lawyer, a factory worker, a Swiss journalist, and a woman who worked with the Jewish resistance—found it hard to believe their descriptions of life and death in Auschwitz.

They told their listeners about the selections at the railroad ramps. They told them about the whips, the prodding rifle butts, and the yelping dogs of the SS. They told them about the starvation diet of thin soup, bread, and tea; the heavy labor assignments; the ever-present lice; and the typhus and dysentery.

The expressions of their listeners indicated that there was too much to digest at once. Wetzler told them about the Nazi doctors who experimented with live prisoners as if they were guinea pigs: "Dr. Mengele is in charge of scientific extermination and personally specialises [sic] in experiments on twins." Wetzler continued to report that other doctors sterilized men and women, injected disease-causing bacteria into the prisoners' bodies, and caused horrible physical

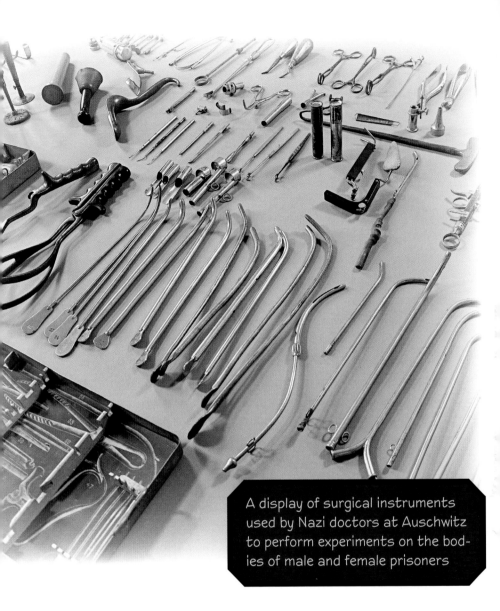

A display of surgical instruments used by Nazi doctors at Auschwitz to perform experiments on the bodies of male and female prisoners

deformities through grotesque surgical procedures. Vrba and Wetzler also submitted the torn label from the canister of Zyklon B pellets.

The meeting ended with a request for Vrba and Wetzler to type up a report, detailing fact by fact everything that they had told their panel of listeners. The underground representatives asked Vrba and Wetzler to provide five or six copies of the report in three days' time. Vrba reacted angrily. Yes, of course they could. They'd work day and night. But each passing day meant the deaths of thousands. Hadn't the panel already heard enough? Hadn't they seen sufficient evidence?

The representatives persuaded Vrba to calm down. They told him that in three days, when the panel reconvened, a very important person would be present: a representative of the International Committee of the Red Cross, the world's oldest private humanitarian organization. Founded in 1863, the Red Cross aids victims of war and natural disasters—the wounded, the sick, and the homeless, including refugees and prisoners of war of all nations. Its headquarters is in Geneva, in neutral Switzerland.

Although the Nazi concentration camps had been in operation since 1933, there was no record, in May 1944, of the Red Cross ever having visited one of them. The organization had accepted assurances from Nazi authorities that the prisoners were being treated fairly. The Red Cross did send food, soap, and clothing parcels to the various camps, but they received no evidence that the aid actually reached the prisoners. Vrba and Wetzler knew firsthand that the SS men either used the Red Cross items themselves or mailed the contents of the packages home to their families in Germany.

Vrba and Wetzler were anxious to confront the Red Cross representative, a man who seemed self-satisfied and appeared almost amused at the extraordinary passion of the two escaped prisoners. The Red Cross parcels came up for discussion, and Wetzler made it clear that even if the aid had reached the prisoners, it would have been of minimal value. The prisoners didn't need alms, he told the man from the Red Cross; they needed freedom. "Don't soothe your conscience with biscuits," he said, "when tons of human flesh are burnt there every day. . . . [I]nform the world . . . and force Hitler to scrap the concentration camps."

The U.S. Army Air Force took reconnaissance photos of Auschwitz-Birkenau starting in April 1944, but never bombed its rail lines.

NORWAY

SWE

North
Sea

DENMARK

Neuengamme
Bergen-Belsen
Esterwegen
NETH.   Dora-
Vught   Mittelbau   GERMAN

BELGIUM   Flessenburg   Ther

Drancy   Buchenwald

Natzweiler   Dachau

FRANCE   SWITZ.   AU
Labo

0   150   300 miles
0   150   300 kilometers

ITALY

■ Concentration camp

Vrba and Wetzler's escape route from Auschwitz to Slovakia (indicated as "Czech" for the country's post-World War II name: Czecho-slovakia): red squares indicate prominent concentration camps built all across Europe with the intention of exterminating its Jewish population.

ESTONIA

RUSSIA

Baltic Sea

Riga
LATVIA

LITHUANIA

Maly
Trostenets

EAST
PRUSSIA
Stutthof

...ck
...ausen

...urg

POLAND

Treblinka

Sobibor

Lublin-Majdanik

...ross-Rosen

Belzec

...kenau

Auschwitz

H.

Escape route

Birkenau
Auschwitz

Vistula R.

Sol R.

POLAND

Bielsko
Biala

Zywiec

Milowka

Cadca
Skalite

CZECH.

Zilina

...hausen

HUNGARY

ROMANIA

Black Sea

Jassenovec

Stara
Gradiska

Zemun

YUGOSLAVIA

BULGARIA

TURKEY

...Sea

Vrba shoved the report that he and Wetzler had written in the direction of their interviewer. He urged the Red Cross man to read its contents—the most detailed description of the camp, the prisoners, and their lives and deaths that anyone had ever brought forth from the killing factory known as Auschwitz-Birkenau.

In a final effort to discredit the Vrba-Wetzler Report, the representative reported that the Red Cross had received denials of any mistreatment in the camps from Joseph Goebbels, the German minister of propaganda, and from the German Red Cross. He also showed them postcards written by camp prisoners stating that they were well and would like to receive food parcels from home.

Vrba and Wetzler knew all about the postcards. In a stinging retort, Wetzler told the Red Cross representative that these were the very cards and letters postdated March 23 to 25, 1944, and that the "quarantined" Theresienstadt Jews at Auschwitz had been ordered to write before they were sent to their deaths on March 7 and 8, 1944.

Informing the United States and Great Britain

Vrba and Wetzler, discouraged at the apparent failure of their mission, were still concealing themselves in Slovakia on June 14, 1944, when word of the Vrba-Wetzler Report went out to the world for the very first time. On that day, the Czech delegate to the League of Nations in Switzerland and the World Jewish Congress jointly sent the following telegram to London: "According report made by two Slovakian Jews who escaped from Birkenau . . . 3,000 Czechoslovakian Jews who were brought from Terezin [Theresienstadt] to Birkenau on December 20, 1943, will be gassed . . . June 20, 1944."

The telegram—which was promptly forwarded to the United States—also announced that the Vrba-Wetzler

Report contained "horrible descriptions of massacres in gas chambers [of] Auschwitz Birkenau of hundreds of thousands [of] Jews [of] all nationalities [in] occupied Europe."

It was too late, of course, to save the Theresienstadt Jews or the numerous others who had been exterminated in the camps. But at least the world media had recognized, finally, the value of witnesses who had endured a Nazi death camp and had escaped to tell about it.

On June 15, the BBC broadcast the news that "London has been informed" and issued the following warning from the British government to the German authorities: "All those responsible for the mass murder . . . shall be brought to account."

In the days and months that followed, excerpts from the Vrba-Wetzler Report appeared in the *New York Times* and many other newspapers worldwide. At last, in November 1944, the U.S. government made the contents of the entire Vrba-Wetzler Report public. The document, issued by the War Refugee Board of the Executive Office of the President, was titled GERMAN EXTERMINATION CAMPS—AUSCHWITZ AND BIRKENAU.

The introduction to the document read, "So revolting and diabolical are the German atrocities that the minds of civilized people find it difficult to believe that they have actually taken place. But the governments of the United States and of other countries have evidence which clearly substantiates the facts."

The Allies stepped up bombings of German cities, and ground troops steadily advanced into German territory. And on January 27, 1945, Soviet troops entered Poland and liberated Auschwitz. The camp, which had been in operation since May 1940 and had been responsible for the extermination of 1.1 million people—90 percent of them Jews—was no longer under Nazi control. On May 7, 1945, Germany surrendered unconditionally, and World War II came to a close in Europe.

The victorious army of the Soviet Union entered Poland from the east and, on January 27, 1945, liberated the prisoners of Auschwitz.

For Vrba and Wetzler, the last months of the war were a troubling time. Yes, they had finally succeeded in informing the great powers about the Nazi death factories. But too many lives had been lost due to six years of disbelief and indifference by the fighting nations, as well as cowardice and betrayal on the part of anti-Nazi leaders. In fall 1944, Vrba and Wetzler again risked their lives. They joined partisans fighting in the mountains of Slovakia for the liberation of their country.

Directly following World War II, from 1945 to 1946, the United States and its allies tried members of the Nazi high command in Nuremberg, Germany. The Vrba-Wetzler Report was used as evidence, as part of a document known as the Auschwitz Protocol, and played an important role in condemning Nazi war criminals to death. Both Vrba and Wetzler, however, were determined to put their eyewitness accounts of Auschwitz-Birkenau into writing for a broad readership and for future generations. In the 1960s, each man published his own gripping story of imprisonment in the notorious death camp.

Rudolf Vrba was born on September 11, 1924. His real name at birth, and as recorded at Auschwitz, was Walter Rosenberg. After he escaped from Auschwitz and joined the partisans, he changed his name to Rudolf Vrba—the name he chose as a freedom fighter rather than a victim—and kept it for the rest of his life. After the war, Vrba earned a doctoral degree as a medical researcher in the Czech capital of Prague. He worked in Israel, Great Britain, Canada, and the United States. In 1963, his autobiography, *I Cannot Forgive* (later retitled *I Escaped from Auschwitz*), was published in London and New York.

Until the early 1990s, Vrba followed a professional career, culminating in a professorship of pharmacology at the University of British Columbia in Canada. He also contributed extensively to the growing body of information on the Holocaust. Rudolf Vrba died on March 27, 2006, in Vancouver, Canada. He was eighty-one years old.

Alfred Wetzler, born May 10, 1918, remained in Czechoslovakia after the war and worked as a journalist and newspaper editor. He wrote under the pseudonym Jozef Lanik, perhaps to protect himself from his former persecutors. Wetzler's book *Escape from Hell*, a narrative of life in Auschwitz and of his and Vrba's escape, was published in Bratislava, Czechoslovakia, in 1964. Its first English translation appeared in 2007. Alfred Wetzler died in Bratislava in 1988.

After the Holocaust

To the credit of Germany, the nation's post–World War II government undertook a broad program of reeducating its citizens and making reparation payments to Holocaust survivors all over the world. It set up memorials in the former concentration camps and established remembrance museums so that no one would forget the Nazis' crimes and their victims.

In 1943, while World War II still raged, an escaped Polish Jew named Raphael Lemkin gave a name to the crime of attempting to exterminate an entire people because of its religion, race, ethnicity, or national background. He called the crime *genocide*, a combination of the Greek words for people, race, or kind ("geno") and kill ("cide").

Adolf Hitler's effort to wipe out Europe's Jews was not the first genocide in recorded history—or even in the 1900s. Only twenty years earlier, the Turkish government's attempt to destroy its minority Armenian population had resulted in 1.5 million deaths. Following the 6 million deaths of the Holocaust, however, many people hoped that no nation, or warring group within a nation, would embark on a campaign to eliminate an entire minority population for reasons of prejudice and intolerance.

Yet the second half of the twentieth century and the start of the twenty-first century saw four such major murderous conflicts. In Cambodia, between 1975 and 1979, the ruthless Khmer Rouge regime of the Maoist communist leader Pol Pot was responsible for 2 million deaths. In the former Yugoslavia, between 1992 and 1995, Serbian Christians killed 100,000 Bosnian Muslims. In Rwanda in 1994, the African Hutu people massacred 800,000 African Tutsi people and moderate Hutus.

In 2003, the Arab Muslim government of Sudan endorsed and funded a violent campaign to destroy the impoverished, "racially different" people of the country's western region of Darfur. The death toll is estimated at 400,000. In all of the foregoing genocides, intervention from other nations occurred either too late or not at all.

By comparison, the bravery and selflessness of Rudolf Vrba and Alfred Wetzler, who risked their lives to escape from Auschwitz and to make the truth known, provide shining examples of the nobility of the human spirit.

TIME LINE

January 30, 1933—Adolf Hitler is appointed chancellor of Germany; Jews number 566,000 in a population of 5.5 million.

April 1, 1933—Nazis begin persecuting Jews with the boycott of shops and businesses.

September 15, 1935—Racist laws deprive Jews of their German citizenship.

March 12–13, 1938—The Nazis annex Austria, which has a Jewish population of 200,000.

November 9–10, 1938—Kristallnacht, the Night of Broken Glass, takes place in Germany and Austria.

September 1, 1939—Nazis invade Poland (which has a Jewish population of 3.35 million, the largest in Europe); World War II begins.

January 25, 1940—The Auschwitz concentration camp in Poland becomes operational.

April 9, 1940—Nazis invade Denmark and Norway, which have Jewish populations of eight thousand and two thousand respectively.

May 10, 1940—Nazis invade France (Jewish population 350,000), Belgium (Jewish population 65,000), Holland (Jewish population 140,000), and Luxembourg (Jewish population 3,500).

December 1941—Japan, Germany's ally, attacks the United States at Pearl Harbor, Hawaii, on December 7; the United States enters World War II against Japan in the Pacific and Germany and Italy in Europe.

April 12, 1942—Alfred Wetzler arrives at Auschwitz.

June 27, 1942—Rudolf Vrba arrives at Auschwitz.

July 17/18, 1942—Heinrich Himmler visits Auschwitz-Birkenau and orders the building of efficient new gas chamber and crematorium units.

September 7, 1943—Transports of Jews from Theresienstadt arrive at Auschwitz to be "quarantined" until they are sent to the gas chambers.

March 19, 1944—The Nazis occupy Hungary, which has a Jewish population of 725,000.

April 7–10, 1944—Vrba and Wetzler enter their hideout in Auschwitz and are reported missing. Three days later they leave their hiding place and set out to reach Slovakia through occupied Poland.

May 15, 1944—The deportation of Hungarian Jews to Auschwitz begins; 550,000 will eventually be exterminated.

June 14–15, 1944—The contents of the Vrba-Wetzler Report are released to Great Britain and the United States.

January 27, 1945—Soviet troops enter Poland and liberate Auschwitz.

April 30, 1945—Hitler commits suicide in his Berlin bunker.

May 7, 1945—Germany surrenders unconditionally, and World War II ends in Europe.

November 20, 1945—The Nuremberg Trials begin; the Vrba-Wetzler Report is used as evidence against Nazi war criminals.

NOTES

Chapter 1

p. 16, par. 1, "slightly mad . . . ": William L. Shirer, *The Rise and Fall of the Third Reich: A History of Nazi Germany* (New York: Simon and Schuster, 1960), p. 29.

p. 18, par. 3 "After a walk of about twenty minutes . . . ": "The Vrba-Wetzler Report," *The Auschwitz Protocol*, www. holocaustresearchproject.org/other camps/auschproto.html (accessed 1/1/2010).

p. 21, par. 5, "Final Solution to the Jewish Question" . . . Shirer, p. 1257.

p. 22, par. 2, "watched the whole process . . . ": Rudolf Vrba, *I Escaped from Auschwitz* (Fort Lee, NJ: Barricade Books, 2002), p. 7.

p. 22, par. 3, "the overcrowded huts . . . ": Rudolf Hoess quoted in Vrba, p. 7.

p. 23, par. 1, "the grossly inefficient . . . ": Vrba, p. 8.

p. 23, par. 2, "The gas chambers . . . ": Vrba, p. 8.

p. 25, par. 1, "Prominent guests from Berlin . . . ": "The Vrba-Wetzler Report."

p. 26, par. 4, "the Jewish world conspiracy.": Shirer, p. 586.

p. 28, par. 3, "men, fourteen to sixty years old . . . ": Martin Gilbert, *Auschwitz and the Allies* (New York: Holt, Reinhart and Winston, 1981), p. 40.

Chapter 2

p. 31, par. 1, "to which we were herded . . . ": "The Vrba-Wetzler Report."

p. 32, par. 2, "we found huge sheds . . . ": "The Vrba-Wetzler Report."

p. 36, par. 4 "trembling hands . . . ": Alfred Wetzler, *Escape from Hell: The True Story of the Auschwitz Protocol* (New York: Berghahn Books, 2007), p. 77.

p. 38, par. 2, "During the week following September 7, 1943 . . . ": "The Vrba-Wetzler Report."

p. 39, par. 2, "Of all these Jews . . . ": "The Vrba-Wetzler Report."

p. 39, par. 5, "If anything comes up . . . ": Wetzler, p. 97.

Chapter 3

p. 48, par. 2, "If you really trust me . . . ": Wetzler, p. 167.

p. 51, par. 3, "Rags . . . ": Wetzler, p. 176.

p. 51, par. 6, "When it gets light . . . ": Wetzler, p. 179.

p. 51, par. 6, "Tell everyone about Auschwitz.": Wetzler, p. 180.

Chapter 4

p. 56, par. 5, "Dr. Mengele is in charge . . . ": Wetzler, p. 202.

p. 58, par. 4, "Don't soothe your conscience . . . ": Wetzler, p. 20.

p. 62, par. 4, "According report made by two Slovakian Jews . . . ": Henryk Swiebocki, ed., *London Has Been Informed* . . . (Oswiecim, Poland: The Auschwitz-Birkenau State Museum, 2008), p. 54.

p. 63, par. 1, "horrible descriptions. . .": Swiebocki, p. 54.

p. 63, par. 3, "All those responsible . . . ": Swiebocki, p. 56.

p. 63, par. 5, "So revolting and diabolical . . . ": Swiebocki, p. 59.

GLOSSARY

anti-Semitism— Prejudice against Jews based on hostility toward their ethnic background, their culture, and/or their religion.

Buna—A Nazi industrial complex near Auschwitz; a subcamp, also known as Auschwitz III, located at Buna.

crematoria—Furnaces for burning dead bodies.

dumdum bullets—Bullets that expand upon impact and inflict large, jagged body wounds.

Gestapo—The secret state police of Nazi Germany.

Holocaust—The Nazis' extermination of 6 million Jews during World War II.

kapo—A concentration camp prisoner entrusted with certain low-ranking duties under SS supervision.

Kristallnacht (Night of Broken Glass)—The nights of November 9 and 10, 1938, when Nazis in Germany and Austria arrested and murdered Jews and destroyed their property on a massive scale.

partisans—In World War II, fighters in a loosely organized military force attempting to free a nation dominated by an enemy force.

propaganda—Ideas or information spread to promote a cause or a belief, such as Nazi Germany's anti-Semitism.

puppet dictator—The leader of a government that is dominated by a larger and more powerful nation led by a dictator, or absolutist ruler.

***Schutzstaffel* (SS)**—The special police force in charge of concentration camps run by Nazi Germany.

Star of David—A six-pointed star, the shield of David, that is a traditional symbol of the Jewish people.

Zyklon B—A cyanide-based pesticide that was introduced in pellet form into the sealed gas chambers of Nazi concentration camps.

FURTHER INFORMATION

BOOKS

Bartoletti, Susan Campbell. *Hitler Youth: Growing Up in Hitler's Shadow*. New York: Scholastic, 2005.

Boyne, John. *The Boy in the Striped Pajamas*. New York: Random House, 2006.

Roy, Jennifer. *Yellow Star*. New York: Marshall Cavendish, 2006.

Spring, Debbie. *The Righteous Smuggler*. Toronto, Canada: Second Story Press, 2006.

Zusak, Markus. *The Book Thief*. New York: Random House, 2006.

WEBSITES

Museum of Jewish Heritage, Battery Park, New York City
The museum opened in 1997 for the purpose of educating people of all ages and backgrounds about the twentieth-century Jewish experience, as well as the 5,000-year-old history of Judaism.

www.mjhnyc.org

Simon Wiesenthal Center, Los Angeles, California
The center was opened in 1977 and was named for Simon Wiesenthal (1908–2005), a survivor of the Nazi death camps.

Wiesenthal dedicated his life to documenting the crimes of Hitler's Germany and to ferreting out nearly 1,100 Nazi war criminals. In addition to having recorded the history of the Holocaust, the Simon Wiesenthal Center maintains an ongoing watch for human rights violations and promotes tolerance worldwide.

www.wiesenthal.com

United States Holocaust Memorial Museum, Washington, D.C.
Dedicated in 1993, the museum is a living memorial to those who lost their lives in the Holocaust. Its purpose is to inspire citizens and national leaders worldwide to confront hatred, promote dignity, and prevent genocide.

www.ushmm.org

BIBLIOGRAPHY

Gilbert, Martin. *Auschwitz and the Allies.* New York: Holt, Rhinehart and Winston, 1981.

Hoess, Rudolf. *Commandant of Auschwitz: The Autobiography of Rudolf Hoess.* London: Phoenix Press, 2000.

Lacqueur, Walter. *The Terrible Secret: Suppression of the Truth about Hitler's "Final Solution."* Boston: Little Brown, 1980.

Shirer, William L. *The Rise and Fall of the Third Reich: A History of Nazi Germany.* New York: Simon and Schuster, 1960.

Smolen, Kazimierz. *Auschwitz 1940–1945: Guidebook Through the Museum.* Katowice, Poland: Krajowa Agencja Wydawnicza, 1981.

Swiebocki, Henryk, ed. *London Has Been Informed . . .* Oswiecim, Poland: The Auschwitz-Birkenau State Museum, 2008.

Vrba, Rudolf. *I Escaped from Auschwitz.* Fort Lee, NJ: Barricade Books, 2002.

Wetzler, Alfred. *Escape from Hell: The True Story of the Auschwitz Protocol.* New York: Berghahn Books, 2007.

Wyman, David S. *Abandonment of the Jews: America and the Holocaust, 1941–1945.* New York: Pantheon, 1984.

INDEX

ABOUT THE AUTHOR

Lila Perl has published more than sixty books, both fiction and nonfiction, for preteen and young adult readers. Recent nonfiction subjects include ancient civilizations, a Holocaust memoir, terrorism, theocracy, and genocide. For her ancient history and Holocaust titles, she has done extensive research abroad, including two visits to the concentration camp of Auschwitz in Poland, most recently in 2009, and visits to Dachau and Buchenwald in Germany.

Two of Perl's books have been honored with American Library Association Notable Awards: *Red-Flannel Hash and Shoo-Fly Pie* and *Four Perfect Pebbles: A Holocaust Story*. Ten titles have been selected as ALA Notable Children's Trade Books in the Field of Social Studies. Perl has also received a Boston Globe Horn Book Award, a Sidney Taylor Committee Award, and a Young Adults' Choice Award from the International Reading Association. The New York Public Library has cited her work among Best Books for the Teen Age. Her most recent book for Marshall Cavendish Benchmark was *Immigration: This Land Is Whose Land?* in its Controversy! series.

Perl lives in Beechhurst, New York.